I CHOOSE
to Try Again

I CHOOSE SERIES

ELIZABETH ESTRADA

I CHOOSE
to Try Again

I CHOOSE SERIES

ELIZABETH ESTRADA

I have many interests.
I like piano and basketball.
But when things get too hard,
Or when I have a big fall,

I don't feel like trying again.
Quitting is usually my **answer**.
It's not worth committing
Because all I can hear is **laughter**.

One day my best friend, Whitney,
Took me aside and **said**,
"Kiara, everything is difficult at first,
But there are easier roads **ahead**."

"When we get back up
We build our brain **muscle**.
If we keep trying,
We'll eventually solve the **puzzle**."

"Not everything is easy,
But always say, 'I **can**!'
And if at first you don't succeed,
Make sure you try **again**."

"It doesn't matter what it is -
Schoolwork, chores, or **sports**.
Study hard and practice,
And remember all that you're **taught**."

"People may say, 'You can't do it,'
Expecting you to **fail**,
But the words, 'I choose to try again,'
Will help you to **prevail**."

"Sometimes we are challenged
When life gets really **rough**,
But let's say, "You won't beat me,
Because I'm super **tough**."

"People may try to put us down
And say, 'You'll achieve **nothing**.'
But we know if we try hard enough
We can do **anything**."

"We won't ever give up on our dreams,
If we fall, we'll get up **again**.
Just try harder every day,
And eventually we'll **win**.

Try not to say 'never.'
That brainwashes you to **fail**.
It means that you won't have the chance
To raise the victory **sail**."

"If there is something that you want
That you just can't **achieve**,
Will you give up trying,
Just pack your bag and **leave**?

Or will you keep on striving
To gain that thing you **need**.
Say, 'I choose to try again,'
Keep aiming to **succeed**."

"Be confident and try your best
For your life has just **begun**.
Until you cross the finish line
The race has not been **won**."

This was a valuable lesson
For me to hear and **understand**.
I promised to get back up,
And always give my trying **hand**.

I made a list of all the goals
I wanted to **achieve**.
If there is one that challenges me,
I'll just roll up my **sleeves**.

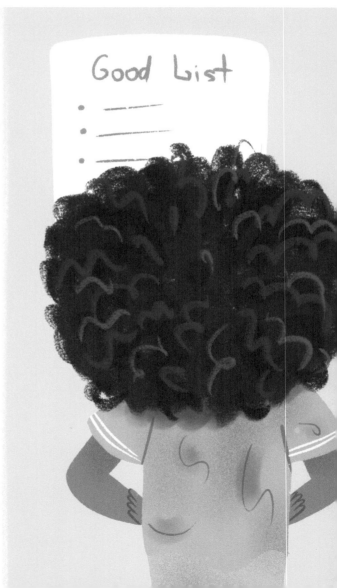

If I fail, I'll try again,
I'll never say, "Too **hard**."
I'll study or practice even more.
I don't even need a **reward**.

I got a "C" in English class.
I didn't want to **fail**.
I decided to study harder
To make sure I'd have it **nailed**.

I tried out for basketball,
But didn't make the **team**.
That just makes me train harder
Until I achieve my **dream**.

I am so determined
To do the best I **can**.
I won't stop when things get tough.
I choose to try again.

Dear Reader,

Thank you to my readers. I hope you enjoyed "I Choose to Try Again." I spent a lot of time developing this book and series.

So please tell me what you liked and even what you disliked. What kind of emotion should be in my next book?

I love to receive messages from my readers. Please write to me at Elizabethestradainfo@gmail.com

I would also greatly appreciate it if you could review my book. Your feedback matters a lot to me!

With love,
Elizabeth

CPSIA information can be obtained
at www.ICGtesting.com
Printed in the USA
LVHW071553131122
733037LV00009B/103

* 9 7 8 1 6 3 7 3 1 2 0 9 4 *